I Can Read!

BEGINNING READING 1

Slugsy's Dinner

HarperCollins *Children's Books*

This is Slugsy.

He lives with Stingo

in a den at the bottom

of Apple Tree House.

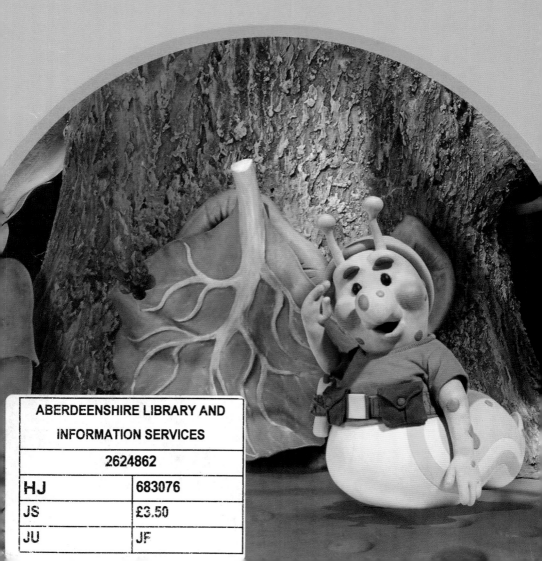

Slugsy loves Primrose
but he is too shy
to tell her.

Slugsy asks Fifi what to do.
"How do I tell Primrose
that I like her, Fifi?"
he says.

"Why not ask her to your house for dinner?" says Fifi.

Here is Primrose.

She lives in Flowertot Cottage
with her best friend, Violet.

Primrose likes everything to be
tidy and clean, and to smell nice.
She does not think
that Slugsy smells nice.

Slugsy goes to Flowertot Cottage
to see Primrose.

He is very shy.

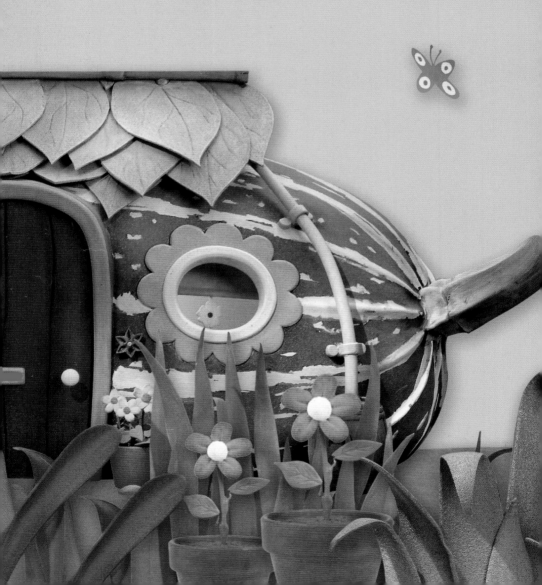

Slugsy brought some flowers
for Primrose.

He knows that she loves flowers.

"Hello, Primrose.

Would you like to come

to my house for dinner today?"

Slugsy asks.

Primrose is very surprised.

She is so happy

to have such pretty flowers

that she says yes to Slugsy.

Slugsy is very happy.

He knows exactly what

he will make for dinner.

First he visits Poppy's stall

to buy vegetables and cheese.

Next, Slugsy takes his shopping
back to his den
to start cooking.

"I hope Primrose likes it!"
thinks Slugsy.

While the dinner is cooking,
Slugsy takes the vegetable scraps
to Diggly's compost heap.

Slugsy doesn't realise that
some smelly old cabbage leaves
have stuck onto him.
He leaves,
smelling of cabbage.

Primrose has washed her petals.

She looks very pretty.

She has also put on some perfume so that she smells nice.

Walking to Slugsy's den,
Primrose smells something
that she does not like.

22

At six o'clock,

Primrose reaches Slugsy's den.

The bad smell

is even worse there.

23

"Hello, Slugsy," says Primrose.
She wonders where
the bad smell is coming from.

"I have made a special dinner
just for you," says Slugsy.
"It is nearly ready.
You can smell it
cooking in the oven."

Primrose is worried

that the bad smell

is the smell of the dinner cooking.

26

"Surprise!" says Slugsy.

Just then, the smelly cabbage leaves

that had been stuck to Slugsy

fly off!

They smell terrible.

Primrose is shocked.

"Slugsy! If you are serving

rotting cabbage leaves

for my dinner,

I will leave right now!"

Slugsy is very embarassed.

"Rotting cabbage leaves?

Where did they come from?"

wonders Slugsy.

Primrose does not want
to hear about Slugsy's cabbage.
"But I have made
cauliflower cheese for our dinner!"
explains Slugsy.

"Cauliflower cheese?"

cries Primrose.

"Why didn't you say so?

I love cauliflower cheese!"

Fifi and the Flowertots is a magazine aimed at 3-5 year olds who love to be busy, just like Fifi. Join the Flowertot fun in Fifi's world!

Talking Fifi
Forget-Me-Not

Have even more Flowertot fun with these Fifi storybooks!

Fun Time Fifi
Interactive Doll

Magic Bubble Mo

A new Bumper Collection is out on DVD now!

Fifi's Tea
Party playset

Visit Fifi at www.fifiandtheflowertots.com